SCIENCE AROUND US

Mammals

By Peter Murray

THE CHILD'S WORLD®
CHANHASSEN, MINNESOTA

The Child's World

Published in the United States of America by The Child's World®
PO Box 326, Chanhassen, MN 55317-0326
800-599-READ
www.childsworld.com

Content Advisers:
Jim Rising, PhD,
Professor of Zoology,
University of Toronto,
Department of Zoology,
Toronto, Ontario,
Canada, and Trudy
Rising, Educational
Consultant, Toronto,
Ontario, Canada

Photo Credits:
Cover/frontispiece: Theo Allofs/Corbis; cover corner: Image 100/Corbis.
Interior: Animals Animals/Earth Scenes: 9 (Paul & Joyce Berquist), 10 (ABPL/Martin
Harvey), 13 (Manoj Shah), 25 (D. Allen Photography), 27 (Gerard Lacz), 29 (OSF/Tim
Shepherd); Corbis: 4, 8 (Wolfgang Kaehler), 15 (John Conrad), 18 (Theo Allofs), 19
(Torleif Svensson); Dembinsky Photo Associates: 11 (Claudia Adams), 16 (Rod Planck),
22 (Mark J. Thomas); Todd Marshall: 7; Photodisc/Punchstock: 12, 21.

The Child's World®: Mary Berendes, Publishing Director

Editorial Directions, Inc.: E. Russell Primm, Editorial Director; Pam Rosenberg, Line
Editor; Katie Marsico, Assistant Editor; Matt Messbarger, Editorial Assistant; Susan
Hindman, Copy Editor; Susan Ashley, Proofreader; Peter Garnham, Terry Johnson,
Olivia Nellums, Katherine Trickle, and Stephen Carl Wender, Fact Checkers; Tim
Griffin/IndexServ, Indexer; Cian Loughlin O'Day, Photo Researcher; Linda S. Koutris,
Photo Selector

The Design Lab: Kathleen Petelinsek, Design and Page Production

Library of Congress Cataloging-in-Publication Data
Murray, Peter, 1952 Sept. 29–
  Mammals / by Peter Murray.
      v. cm. — (Science around us)
Includes bibliographical references (p.   ).
Contents: The mammal in the mirror—The first mammals—What makes a mammal
a mammal?—Mammal types : insectivores, rodents, and bats—Types of mammals :
hooves, flippers, and pouches—Types of mammals : meat-eaters and monkeys.
  ISBN 1-59296-216-5 (lib. bdg. : alk. paper) 1. Mammals—Juvenile literature.
[1. Mammals.] I. Title. II. Science around us (Child's World (Firm))
  QL706.2.M87 2004
  599—dc22   2003027219

TABLE OF CONTENTS

CHAPTER ONE

THE MAMMAL IN THE MIRROR

Look in a mirror. What do you see? You see a head with two eyes, a nose, two ears, and a mouth.

Your head is covered with tens of thousands of fine, tough threads called hair. Each eyelid has a fringe of short hairs. There is hair growing inside your nose. Look closely, and you will see thousands of tiny hairs all over your body.

When you look in a mirror, a mammal looks back—you!

Back away and look at the rest of yourself in the mirror. You have four limbs and a flexible backbone. Put your hand on your cheek. It feels warm. You are warm-blooded—an endotherm.

If a mouse or a monkey looked at itself in the mirror, it would see pretty much the same thing: a hairy, warm-blooded, four-limbed animal. Even elephants and whales have hair, although it is not always obvious. Mice, monkeys, elephants, whales, and humans are all mammals.

There are more than 4,000 **species** of mammals on Earth, from the gigantic blue whale to human beings to the tiniest shrew. All mammals have certain things in common, but every species is unique.

Mammals are a type of vertebrate, or animal with a backbone. Fish, amphibians, reptiles, and birds are also vertebrates. What makes mammals different from the others? Are we nothing more than hairy, warm-blooded reptiles?

CHAPTER TWO

THE FIRST MAMMALS

Three hundred million years ago, the land was ruled by reptiles. Some were large and lumbering; others were small and quick. Over tens of millions of years, reptile groups **evolved** into different forms. Some grew shells to become the turtles. Others grew long and toothy to become the first crocodiles. One group of quick, agile lizards rose up on two legs and became the dinosaurs. But another group of small reptiles developed a new type of hairlike scale that kept them warm. Those small, furry reptiles became the first mammals.

The first mammals were small, warm-blooded **insectivores.** In a world filled with hungry reptiles, the early mammals survived by being small and probably by hiding during the day.

Warm-blooded animals such as mammals and birds have one

Eotyrannus was just one of the many reptiles that lived on Earth millions of years ago.

great advantage over the cold-blooded reptiles. When the tempera-

ture drops, so does a reptile's body temperature. They become slug-

gish. In the cool of the night, they hunker down and wait for the

sun to rise again. However, the early mammals, with their warm-

blooded **metabolism** and insulating layer of hair, could hunt

their insect prey at night, when the reptiles were inactive.

Reptiles, such as this panther chameleon, are cold-blooded. That means their body temperature rises and falls with the temperature of the air or water around them.

*Warm-blooded, furry mammals, such as this desert rat,
can hunt insects at night when reptiles are sleeping.*

For about 150 million years, these small mammals survived in a
world ruled by dinosaurs and other reptiles. It was not until the
dinosaurs died out about 65 million years ago that mammals began
to evolve into the many and varied forms we know today.

CHAPTER THREE

WHAT MAKES A MAMMAL A MAMMAL?

HAIR

All mammals have hair or fur at some stage of their lives. Hair is made of keratin, the same hard, flexible material that makes up your fingernails, a rhino's horn, or a reptile's scales. But hair is a much better insulator than scales. The thick fur of a lynx keeps it warm during the cold northern winter. A porcupine has long, stiff, sharp hairs called quills that protect it from **predators.** The sea

The horn of the black rhinoceros and human finger-nails are made of the same material—keratin.

otter has a thick coat of more than a billion fine, waterproof hairs that keeps it warm and dry in the water.

TEETH

Reptiles, amphibians, and fish all have teeth. Only mammals, however, have a variety of different teeth to do different jobs. In humans, the front teeth, or incisors, are flat with sharp edges—good for biting into an apple. On either side of the incisors are the canine teeth, used for biting and tearing meat. In back are the molars, or grinding teeth. Having a variety of teeth means that humans can eat many different kinds of food.

The long, stiff hairs of a porcupine are called quills. They help keep the porcupine safe from predators.

Polar bears live in the Arctic regions of the world. They have thick, white fur that helps keep them warm.

BODY TEMPERATURE

Mammals and birds are the only warm-blooded vertebrates—their body temperature does not change with the weather. Being warm-blooded gives mammals the ability to live almost anywhere on the planet. This may be one of the reasons mammals survived when the dinosaurs died out.

BEHAVIOR

Most reptiles and amphibians never see their offspring. They simply lay their eggs and walk away. Mammals are different. They give birth to live babies, and they care for their young.

A cheetah cub stays with its mother for about 18 months after it is born.

Baby mammals are born helpless. They can't find their own food. For the first part of its life, a baby mammal lives on its mother's milk. Mammals are the only animals that produce milk. Some young mammals spend only a short time with their parents. Baby mice are fed by their mothers for about three weeks before setting off on their own. By six weeks of age, they are having their own babies.

The platypus, a small aquatic mammal, does not give birth to live young. It lays eggs! The echidna, or spiny anteater, is the only other egg-laying mammal.

Elephants mature much more slowly. They don't eat solid food until they are six months old and don't become full-grown adults until they are about 13 years old.

Human beings take longer than any other mammal to reach maturity. We are eating on our own by the time we are two years old, but we rely on our parents for many more years.

Unlike reptiles, most mammals must be taught how to survive.

Reptiles are born with powerful instincts that tell them how to find food and shelter. Mammal behavior, like that of many birds, is too complex to be regulated by instinct alone.

A mother fox must

Mammal mothers teach their young how to survive. A fox kit must be taught how to hunt by its mother.

teach her babies, called kits, to hunt. Baby deer learn from their mothers when to run and hide, and how to find food. Young humans must be taught how to use language and tools.

Mammals also learn by playing. Play is how young mammals learn to use their bodies. It is how they grow strong and how they learn to get along with one another.

CHAPTER FOUR

INSECTIVORES, RODENTS, AND BATS

INSECTIVORES

Mammals have been gobbling up insects for more than 200 million years. Shrews, our smallest insectivores, probably look a lot like the mammals that lived during the age of the dinosaurs. Other insectivores include moles, hedgehogs, and anteaters.

Some scientists believe that the mammals that lived during the time of the dinosaurs probably looked a lot like this shrew.

RODENTS

More than one-third of all animal

species are rodents. Mice, rats, lem-

A rodent's teeth grow throughout its life. It has to keep gnawing, or its teeth will grow too long for its mouth.

mings, and beavers all belong to this group. Rodents live almost every-

where on Earth—you might have some living in your house right

now! Rodents have sharp, strong incisor teeth. They use their teeth to

bite through bark, seeds, leaves, and other plant matter.

Phoberomys pattersoni, an **extinct** relative of the guinea pig,

was the largest rodent that ever lived. It was about the size of a cow.

BATS

You probably don't see a bat very often, but these flying mammals

are common everywhere. There are nearly 1,000 species of bats.

Among mammals, only rodents are more numerous.

All bats are nocturnal, meaning they come out only at night.

Bats, such as these flying foxes, are the only mammals that can fly.

During the day, bats hide in caves, hollow trees, and attics—just about anywhere they can find a warm, dark place to sleep.

Most bats in North America feed on moths, beetles, mosquitoes, and other flying insects. In warm climates, some bat species use their long tongues to feed on sweet flower nectar. The largest bats, called flying foxes, are fruit eaters, as are most bats that live in the tropics. Some of them have a nearly $1^1/_2$-meter (5-foot) wingspan. Flying foxes can be found in Southeast Asia and Australia.

The vampire bats of South America feed on cattle or chicken blood. They make a small bite with their razor-sharp teeth, then lap up the blood that oozes out. Usually, the victims never know they've been bitten.

CHAPTER FIVE

HOOVES, FLIPPERS, AND POUCHES

HOOFED MAMMALS AND ELEPHANTS

Hoofed mammals are found wherever plant life is abundant.

This group of mammals includes deer, rhinoceroses,

camels, and giraffes. Farm animals such as sheep, pigs, cattle,

Giraffes are the tallest land mammals in the world.

and horses also belong to this group.

Hoofed mammals are **herbivores.**
Giraffes, the tallest of all animals, eat leaves
and shoots from high branches. Hippo-
potamuses spend most of their time in the water, feeding on river
grasses. Many deer live in the woods, feeding on grasses, leaves, fruit,
and tender bark.

Most hoofed mammals are fast runners. They have to be able to
outrun large **carnivores** such as lions and wolves. Only the
largest hoofed mammals, such as adult rhinos and hippos, are safe
from predators.

Elephants, which weigh up to 6,800 kilograms (15,000
pounds), are the biggest of all land animals. Elephants are found in
Africa, India, and Southeast Asia.

SEA MAMMALS

Mammals originally evolved on land, but some mammals have **adapted** to life in the water. Over tens of millions of years, their bodies have changed. Instead of legs and feet, they have flippers. Many sea mammals lose their hair after they are born. They rely on a thick layer of fat to keep themselves warm.

Seals and walruses live along the coasts of every continent. In the water, they are graceful and swift. To sleep, they use their flippers to drag themselves out of the water and find a comfortable place to rest.

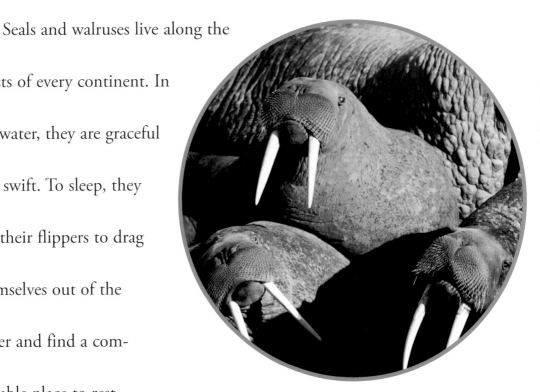

A layer of blubber, or fat, about 15 centimeters (6 inches) thick helps keep walruses warm.

Seals and walruses feed on fish and other small ocean creatures.

Manatees and dugongs look like big, slow, lumpy seals. They live

in warm, shallow coastal areas, where they graze on water plants.

Because manatees move so slowly, they are

often injured by powerboats.

Whales and dolphins look like giant

The blue whale is the largest animal ever to live on Earth. Blue whales can grow to 30 meters (98 feet) long and weigh more than 136,000 kilograms (300,000 pounds)— as much as 20 elephants!

The large, slow-moving manatee lives near warm coastal waters.
Long ago, sailors sometimes thought that manatees were mermaids.

fish, but they are warm-blooded, air-breathing mammals. Like other mammals, they give birth to live young. The babies are born underwater. The first thing they do after they are born is swim to the surface for their first breath of air.

MARSUPIALS

Most of the native mammals of Australia are marsupials, or pouched animals. Marsupial babies are born small, blind, naked, and helpless. A newborn kangaroo is only about the size of a peanut. The newborn must crawl up its mother's belly to her pouch. Inside the pouch, the baby kangaroo, or joey, finds warmth, protection, and milk. For the next year, the joey stays in its mother's pouch.

There are about 280 marsupial species, including kangaroos, Tasmanian devils, and koalas. All modern marsupials live in Australia or New Guinea, except for opossums, which live in the Americas.

CHAPTER SIX

MEAT EATERS AND MONKEYS

CARNIVORES

Carnivores are meat-eating animals such as lions, wolves, bears, and wolverines. They must catch and kill their food before they can eat it, so most carnivores have sharp teeth and claws, fast reflexes, and keen senses.

Cats are among the swiftest and deadliest carnivores. Tigers, leopards, and even common housecats are built for stalking and killing other animals.

The leopard is one of the most powerful cats. After killing a large animal such as an antelope, leopards have been known to drag the dead animal up a tree to keep the food away from other predators.

The dog family includes wolves, foxes, coyotes, and domesticated dogs. Wolves are pack hunters. They team up to bring down large prey such as deer or moose. Tens of thousands of years ago, wolf cubs were first

Leopards are carnivores and will eat any meat they can find, including monkeys, antelope, giraffes, lizards, large birds, and porcupines.

captured and tamed by early humans. All domestic dogs are descended from wolves.

The grizzly bear is the largest land carnivore. Grizzlies and other bears feed on a wide variety of foods, from deer to fish to wild berries.

Skunks, otters, wolverines, and weasels are closely related. They are members of the mustelid family. These carnivores are known for their powerful odors. Some mustelids, such as mink and sable, are valued for their soft, thick fur.

PRIMATES

Monkeys, apes, lemurs, and human beings are all primates. Most primates have long, flexible limbs, **opposable** thumbs, and large brains. Most spend time with others of their kind, and they eat a wide variety of foods.

Monkeys live in Africa, Asia, and South America. The apes—gorillas, chimpanzees, orangutans, and gibbons—live in Africa and Southeast Asia. Lemurs live on Madagascar and the Comoro Islands, off the southeast coast of Africa. Some kinds of lemurs are among the smallest primates—the lesser mouse lemur weighs less than 110 grams (4 ounces).

To find the most successful primate species, go back to that mirror. There it is—the most widespread species on the planet.

Human beings have explored the oceans, the highest mountains, and the driest deserts. We have been to the moon and might one day visit other planets. Like our mammal relatives, we have learned to adapt to a changing, dangerous, and always fascinating world.

A ring tailed lemur will carry her young in her mouth until they are strong enough to hang on to the fur on her back or stomach.

GLOSSARY

adapted (a-DAP-ted) If an animal has adapted, its body or behavior have changed over time to help it survive.

carnivores (KAR-nuh-vors) Carnivores are animals that eat meat.

endangered (en-DAIN-jurd) A plant or animal that is endangered is in danger of becoming extinct.

evolved (ih-VOLVED) Something that has evolved has changed slowly over time.

extinct (ek-STINGKT) If a kind of living thing is extinct, there are no more of them living on Earth.

herbivores (HUR-buh-vors) Herbivores are animals that eat plants.

insectivores (in-SEK-tuh-vors) Insectivores are animals that eat insects.

metabolism (muh-TAB-uh-liz-um) Metabolism is the process by which animals change the food they eat into the energy they need to carry out all their bodily functions.

opposable (uh-PO-zuh-buhl) If a thumb is opposable, then an animal can touch the tip of one or more of its other fingers with it.

predators (PRED-uh-turz) Predators are animals that hunt other animals for food.

species (SPEE-sheez) A species is a type of living thing. Members of the same species can mate and produce young.

DID YOU KNOW?

▶ Sea otters were once hunted almost to extinction for their fine pelts.

▶ The pygmy shrew is only about 4 centimeters (1.5 inches) long and weighs less than a dime. The giant anteater of South America is about 2 meters (6 feet) long.

▶ Capybaras are the largest living rodents. A large capybara can weigh more than 45 kilograms (100 pounds).

▶ Bat wings look like hands with long, skinny fingers. A thin, leathery membrane is stretched between the "fingers."

▶ The thylacine, or Tasmanian tiger, was a wolflike marsupial that once lived all across Australia. The last thylacines died in the 1930s.

A tiny pygmy shrew eats an earthworm.

THE ANIMAL KINGDOM

VERTEBRATES

fish

amphibians

reptiles

birds

mammals

INVERTEBRATES

sponges

worms

insects

spiders & scorpions

mollusks & crustaceans

sea stars

sea jellies

HOW TO LEARN MORE ABOUT MAMMALS

At the Library

Green, Jen. *Mammals.*
Austin, Tex.: Raintree Steck-Vaughn, 2002.

Morgan, Ben. *DK Guide to Mammals.*
New York: DK Publishing, 2003.

Unwin, Mike. *The Life Cycle of Mammals.*
Chicago: Heinemann Library, 2003.

On the Web

VISIT OUR HOME PAGE FOR LOTS OF LINKS ABOUT MAMMALS:
http://www.childsworld.com/links.html
Note to Parents, Teachers, and Librarians: We routinely check our Web links to make sure they're safe, active sites—so encourage your readers to check them out!

Places to Visit or Contact

BROOKFIELD ZOO
To see and learn more about many different kinds of mammals
3300 Golf Road
Brookfield, IL 60513
708/485-0263

SMITHSONIAN NATIONAL MUSEUM OF NATURAL HISTORY
To see the Fossil Mammals exhibit and learn more about how mammals evolved
10th Street and Constitution Avenue NW
Washington, DC 20560
202/357-2700

INDEX

About the Author

Peter Murray has written more than 80 children's books on science, nature, history, and other topics. An animal lover, Pete lives in Golden Valley, Minnesota, in a house with one woman, two poodles, several dozen spiders, thousands of microscopic dust mites, and an occasional mouse.